The Ultimate Guide To Breeding Ball Pythons

Mastering The Art Of Reptile Husbandry: A Comprehensive Handbook For Breeding Ball Pythons

Ethan Harry

Table of Contents

CHAPTER ONE

INTRODUCTION
Welcome to Ball Python Breeding

Welcome to the fascinating world of ball python breeding! If you're here, it's likely because you have a passion for these amazing reptiles and want to learn more about how to breed them successfully. Ball pythons (Python regius) are one of the most popular pet snakes due to their manageable size, relatively docile nature, and the vast array of beautiful color and pattern morphs available. Breeding ball pythons can be a rewarding and educational experience, whether you're a hobbyist looking to expand your collection or an aspiring breeder aiming to produce unique and stunning snakes.

Breeding ball pythons is not only about producing more snakes but also about contributing to the understanding and conservation of these creatures. By learning how to breed them responsibly, you can help ensure healthy, genetically diverse populations in captivity, which can, in turn, reduce the demand for wild-caught specimens.

Why Breed Ball Pythons?

There are several reasons why people choose to breed ball pythons:

1. Passion and Interest: Many breeders start simply because they love these snakes and want to learn more about their behaviors, genetics, and

care. The process of breeding can deepen your understanding and appreciation of these fascinating reptiles.

2. Genetics and Morphs: Ball pythons come in a stunning variety of color and pattern morphs, resulting from different genetic combinations. Breeding allows you to experiment with these genetics and create new, unique morphs. This aspect of breeding can be particularly exciting and rewarding for those interested in reptile genetics.

3. Conservation: Responsible breeding in captivity helps reduce the pressure on wild populations. By producing healthy captive-bred specimens, you contribute to

conservation efforts by providing an alternative to wild-caught snakes.

4. Educational Opportunities: Breeding ball pythons can be an educational experience, offering insights into reptile biology, genetics, and husbandry. It can also be a great way to engage others, especially young enthusiasts, in learning about reptiles and their care.

5. Financial Incentives: While not the primary motivation for most breeders, successful breeding can also have financial benefits. High-demand morphs and healthy, well-cared-for snakes can be sold to other enthusiasts and breeders, potentially covering the costs

of your breeding projects and even providing some profit.

Overview of the Breeding Process

Breeding ball pythons is a multi-step process that requires careful planning, preparation, and attention to detail. Here's an overview of the key stages involved:

1. Choosing Your Breeding Stock: Selecting healthy, genetically diverse, and morphologically interesting snakes is the first step. It's essential to ensure that both the male and female are in good health and have the traits you desire to pass on to their offspring.

2. Setting Up the Environment: Proper housing is crucial for the health and well-being of your ball pythons. This

includes appropriate enclosure sizes, heating, lighting, and humidity control. A stable and stress-free environment helps ensure successful breeding.

3. Pre-Breeding Conditioning: Before introducing the male and female, both snakes need to be in optimal condition. This involves a period of increased feeding to ensure they have adequate fat reserves. It's also essential to monitor their health closely and address any issues before breeding.

4. Introducing the Breeding Pair: Once the snakes are in peak condition, they can be introduced for breeding. Observing their behaviors and ensuring they are compatible is vital. This stage

may require patience, as not all pairs will mate immediately.

5.   Egg Laying and Incubation: After successful mating, the female will eventually lay eggs. Providing a proper nesting environment is crucial. Once the eggs are laid, they need to be carefully incubated under controlled temperature and humidity conditions to ensure healthy development.

6.   Hatching and Neonate Care: As the eggs near hatching, monitoring them becomes even more critical. Once the hatchlings emerge, they require specific care to ensure they thrive. This includes setting up appropriate enclosures, monitoring their first sheds, and ensuring they start feeding properly.

7. Record Keeping and Analysis: Keeping detailed records of breeding pairs, mating dates, egg laying, and hatching is essential. This information helps you track genetic outcomes, improve your breeding strategies, and maintain the health and well-being of your snakes.

CHAPTER TWO

UNDERSTANDING BALL PYTHONS

Natural Habitat and Behavior

Ball pythons (Python regius) are native to the grasslands, savannas, and forests of West and Central Africa. These snakes are typically found in countries such as Ghana, Togo, Benin, and Nigeria. In their natural habitat, they live in areas with plenty of cover, like burrows, termite mounds, and dense vegetation, which provide them with shelter and protection from predators.

Ball pythons are primarily nocturnal, meaning they are most active at night. During the day, they usually hide in burrows or other secluded spots to avoid the heat and potential threats. They are known for their relatively docile nature and tendency to coil into a tight ball when threatened, which is where they get their common name. This defensive behavior helps protect their head and vital organs from predators.

In the wild, ball pythons feed on a variety of small mammals and birds. They are ambush predators, relying on their camouflage to blend into their surroundings and wait for unsuspecting prey to come close. When a suitable target approaches, the python strikes quickly, using its sharp teeth to grasp the prey and then constricts it until it suffocates.

Anatomy and Physiology

Ball pythons are medium-sized snakes, with adults typically ranging from 3 to 5 feet in length, although some individuals can grow longer. They have a robust, muscular body, a short, blunt head, and smooth scales. Their coloration in the wild is usually brown or black with lighter blotches, providing excellent camouflage in their natural environment.

The anatomy of ball pythons includes several key features:

1. Head and Senses: Ball pythons have a well-developed sense of smell, which they use to detect prey and navigate their environment. They have heat-sensing pits along their upper lip

that allow them to detect the body heat of warm-blooded animals, aiding in hunting at night. Their eyes are adapted for low light conditions, and they use their forked tongue to collect scent particles and deliver them to the Jacobson's organ in the roof of their mouth for analysis.

2.   Skin and Scales: The skin of a ball python is covered in scales, which help protect it from environmental hazards and retain moisture. They shed their skin periodically as they grow, a process known as ecdysis.

3.   Skeleton and Muscles: Ball pythons have a flexible spine made up of numerous vertebrae and ribs, allowing them to move smoothly and constrict

prey. Their muscular bodies are designed for powerful constriction, essential for subduing prey.

4. Digestive System: After constricting and swallowing their prey whole, ball pythons rely on strong stomach acids and enzymes to break down the meal. They can go weeks or even months without food, depending on the size of their last meal.

5. Reproductive System: Male and female ball pythons have different reproductive organs. Males have hemipenes (paired reproductive organs), while females have a single reproductive tract. During mating, the male inserts one of his hemipenes into the female to fertilize her eggs.

Common Morphs and Genetics

One of the most fascinating aspects of ball pythons is the wide variety of color and pattern morphs that have been developed through selective breeding. These morphs result from genetic mutations that affect pigmentation, pattern, and sometimes physical structure. Understanding the basics of genetics can help breeders predict and produce desired morphs.

Here are some of the common genetic terms and concepts related to ball python breeding:

1.	Genes and Alleles: Genes are units of heredity that determine specific traits, such as color or pattern. Alleles are different versions of a gene. Ball pythons inherit one allele from each parent for every gene.

2.   Dominant,   Co-Dominant,   and Recessive Traits:

a.   Dominant Traits: Only one copy of the dominant allele is needed for the trait to be expressed. For example, the Spider morph is dominant, meaning if a snake has one Spider allele, it will display the Spider pattern.

b.   Co-Dominant Traits: Both alleles can be expressed simultaneously. An example is the Pastel morph, where a snake with one Pastel allele will show the Pastel coloration, and a snake with two Pastel alleles (a Super Pastel) will have an even more intense version of the trait.

c.	Recessive Traits: A trait is only expressed if the snake inherits two recessive alleles. The Albino morph is recessive, so a snake must have two Albino alleles to display the albino coloration.

3.	Heterozygous and Homozygous:

a.	Heterozygous (Het): The snake has one normal allele and one allele for a specific trait but does not visibly show the trait. For example, a Het Albino carries one albino gene but looks normal.

b.	Homozygous: The snake has two identical alleles for a trait and expresses that trait. For instance, a snake with two Albino alleles is homozygous for the albino trait and will appear albino.

Some popular ball python morphs include:

a.   Albino: Lack of melanin, resulting in white and yellow coloration with red eyes.

b.   Piebald: White patches with normal coloration, creating a striking contrast.

c.   Pastel: Enhanced coloration with brighter yellows and reduced black pigmentation.

d.   Spider: Web-like pattern with reduced side markings.

e.   Clown: Reduced pattern with distinctive head markings and bright coloration.

CHAPTER THREE

GETTING STARTED

Choosing Your Ball Pythons

Choosing the right ball pythons is the first crucial step in your breeding journey. You'll want to select healthy, well-established snakes with desirable traits. Here's what to consider:

1.   Health and Condition: Ensure that both the male and female are in excellent health. Look for clear eyes, smooth skin, and active behavior. Avoid snakes with signs of illness such as respiratory issues, mites, or poor body condition.

2.   Age and Size: Ball pythons should be mature before breeding. Females are typically ready at around 3 years old and

a weight of at least 1,500 grams, while males can be ready slightly younger and lighter, around 1 year old and 700 grams.

3.   Genetics and Morphs: Decide what morphs or genetic traits you are interested in. Choose snakes that carry these traits, whether they are dominant, co-dominant, or recessive. Understanding the genetics of your snakes will help you predict the potential outcomes of your breeding projects.

4.   Temperament: While not as critical as health or genetics, a calm and manageable temperament can make handling and breeding your snakes easier.

By carefully selecting your breeding stock, you'll lay a strong foundation for a successful breeding program.

SETTING UP THE BREEDING ENVIRONMENT

Creating the right environment for your ball pythons is essential for their health and breeding success. This includes choosing the right enclosure, maintaining proper heating and lighting, and ensuring the right humidity and substrate.

Enclosure Types and Sizes

1.　Enclosure Types: Ball pythons can be housed in various types of enclosures, including glass tanks, plastic tubs, and custom-built vivariums. Each type has its advantages:

a. Glass Tanks: Offer excellent visibility and are aesthetically pleasing, but they can be challenging to maintain the right humidity.

b. Plastic Tubs: Retain humidity well and are easy to clean, making them popular for breeding setups.

c. Custom Vivariums: Provide a more naturalistic environment and can be designed to meet specific needs, though they require more effort to set up and maintain.

2. Size: The enclosure should be appropriately sized for the snake's length. A common guideline is that the enclosure's length should be at least one-third of the snake's length. For breeding, ensure the enclosure is

spacious enough to house both the male and female during mating.

Heating and Lighting

1.   Heating: Ball pythons are ectothermic, meaning they rely on external heat sources to regulate their body temperature. Provide a temperature gradient in the enclosure with a warm side (88-92°F) and a cool side (78-82°F). Use under-tank heaters, heat mats, or heat tapes controlled by a thermostat to maintain consistent temperatures.

2.   Lighting: While ball pythons do not require special lighting, maintaining a regular day-night cycle is beneficial. Use a simple light timer to simulate a natural

photoperiod, typically 12 hours of light and 12 hours of darkness.

Humidity and Substrate

1.   Humidity: Ball pythons thrive in humidity levels between 50-60%. Use a hygrometer to monitor humidity levels and mist the enclosure as needed. Higher humidity (up to 70%) may be required during shedding periods.

2.   Substrate: Choose a substrate that helps maintain humidity and is easy to clean. Popular options include:

a.   Cypress Mulch: Retains moisture well and provides a natural look.

b.   Coconut Husk: Good for humidity and odor control.

c.   Paper Towels/Newspaper: Easy to clean and inexpensive, though it doesn't hold humidity as well.

d.   Aspen Bedding: Suitable for drier conditions but may not hold humidity well.

A well-maintained enclosure with proper heating, lighting, humidity, and substrate will keep your ball pythons healthy and ready for breeding.

Feeding and Nutrition

Proper nutrition is vital for the health of your ball pythons and the success of your breeding efforts. Here's how to ensure they are well-fed:

1.   Diet: Ball pythons are carnivores, primarily feeding on rodents. Provide appropriately sized prey items, such as

mice or rats, that are about the same width as the snake's widest part. Feeding frozen-thawed rodents is generally safer and more convenient than live prey.

2.   Feeding Schedule: Juveniles should be fed once a week, while adults can be fed every 1-2 weeks. During the breeding season, it's often beneficial to increase feeding frequency slightly to ensure both the male and female are in prime condition.

3.   Nutritional Health: Monitor the snake's body condition to ensure they are neither underweight nor overweight. A healthy ball python should have a rounded, muscular body with no visible spine or ribs.

4. Supplementing Diet: Generally, a diet of rodents provides all the necessary nutrients. However, ensuring a varied diet with different types of rodents can help cover any nutritional gaps.

5. Water: Always provide a clean, fresh water source. Ball pythons will drink regularly and may also soak in their water dish, especially during shedding.

CHAPTER FOUR

BREEDING PREPARATION

Before diving into the breeding process, it's essential to prepare your ball pythons adequately. This involves ensuring their health, conditioning them properly, and recognizing when they are ready to breed. Careful preparation increases the chances of a successful breeding season and healthy offspring.

Health Checks and Quarantine Procedures

The first step in breeding preparation is to conduct thorough health checks and follow quarantine procedures for any new snakes. This ensures that all your snakes are healthy and reduces the risk of spreading diseases.

1.	Health Checks: Regular health assessments are crucial. Look for signs of illness such as:

a.	Respiratory Issues: Wheezing, bubbling around the nostrils, or open-mouth breathing.

b.	Parasites: Check for mites, ticks, or internal parasites, which can cause weight loss, lethargy, and poor shedding.

c.	General Condition: Ensure your snakes have clear eyes, healthy skin, and a good body condition without visible spine or ribs.

If you notice any health issues, consult a reptile veterinarian for diagnosis and treatment.

2.   Quarantine Procedures: When introducing new snakes to your collection, quarantine them for at least 60-90 days. During this period:

a.   Separate Enclosure: Keep the new snakes in separate enclosures away from your main collection.

b.   Monitor Health: Regularly check for signs of illness or parasites.

c.   Prevent Cross-Contamination: Use separate equipment and wash hands thoroughly between handling different groups of snakes.

Quarantine helps prevent the introduction of diseases to your established snakes, ensuring a healthy breeding environment.

Once your snakes are healthy and cleared from quarantine, you can start conditioning them for breeding. This involves adjusting their feeding regimen and environment to prepare them physically and mentally for the breeding process.

Feeding Regimen

1. Increased Feeding: About 2-3 months before the breeding season, increase the feeding frequency and size of meals for both males and females. This helps build up their fat reserves and ensures they have enough energy for breeding.

a. Females: Feed them every 5-7 days with slightly larger prey items. Aim to get them to a healthy weight of at least 1,500 grams.

b.   Males: Feed them every 7-10 days, as they typically do not require as much weight gain as females. A weight of around 700 grams is usually sufficient.

2.   Healthy Prey: Ensure the prey items are nutritious and appropriately sized. Frozen-thawed rodents are generally recommended for safety and convenience.

3.   Monitoring: Keep a close eye on their weight and overall health. Avoid overfeeding, which can lead to obesity and other health issues.

Environmental Adjustments

Adjusting the environment can help simulate natural conditions and trigger breeding behaviors.

1.   Temperature Cycling: Gradually lower the temperatures in the enclosure to mimic seasonal changes. This can help stimulate breeding behaviors.

a.   Daytime Temperatures: Maintain a warm side at around 85-88°F and a cool side at 78-80°F.

b.   Nighttime Temperatures: Reduce nighttime temperatures by a few degrees, aiming for around 75-78°F.

2.   Light Cycling: Adjust the light cycle to simulate shorter days, which can help trigger breeding. A 10-12 hour light cycle is often effective.

3. Humidity: Maintain humidity levels between 50-60%. Increase humidity slightly during shedding periods or if you notice any respiratory issues.

By optimizing the feeding regimen and environmental conditions, you'll help ensure your snakes are in prime condition for breeding.

Recognizing Breeding Readiness

Understanding when your snakes are ready to breed is crucial for timing introductions and ensuring successful mating.

1. Physical Signs: Look for physical indicators that your snakes are ready to breed.

a.   Females: They should be of adequate weight (at least 1,500 grams) and exhibit a healthy body condition. You may also notice increased activity or roaming behavior as they search for a mate.

b.   Males: Males should also be of sufficient weight (around 700 grams) and may show signs of increased activity or interest in the female's enclosure.

2.   Behavioral Signs: Both males and females will exhibit specific behaviors when they are ready to breed.

a.   Females: Increased roaming and restless behavior are common signs that a female is ready to breed. She may also spend more time near the cool end of the enclosure.

b.   Males: Males may become more active and start "pulsing" or twitching when in close proximity to a female. They may also exhibit courtship behaviors such as rubbing their heads against the female.

3.   Introductions: When both snakes show signs of readiness, introduce the male to the female's enclosure. Monitor their interactions closely.

a.   Positive Signs: The male will typically start courting the female, which includes tail-wagging and alignment of their bodies. The female may respond by lifting her tail, allowing the male to copulate.

b.   Negative Signs: If either snake shows aggression or disinterest, separate them and try again later.

CHAPTER FIVE

THE BREEDING PROCESS

Successfully breeding ball pythons involves introducing the breeding pair, observing courtship and mating behaviors, and monitoring mating success. Here's a detailed yet straightforward guide to help you through each step.

Introducing the Breeding Pair

Once your ball pythons are conditioned and show signs of breeding readiness, it's time to introduce the male to the female's enclosure. This process requires careful observation and patience.

1. Timing: Introduce the male to the female's enclosure during the breeding

season, typically from late fall to early spring. This timing coincides with their natural breeding period in the wild.

2.   Environment: Ensure the enclosure provides a stress-free environment. Maintain appropriate temperature gradients, humidity levels, and provide hiding spots. Both snakes should feel secure and comfortable.

3.   Introduction: Gently place the male into the female's enclosure, preferably during the evening when ball pythons are more active. Observe their initial interactions closely to ensure there is no aggression.

4.   Initial Observation:

a.   Positive Signs: If the male starts to explore and shows interest in the female by rubbing against her or aligning his body with hers, it's a good sign.

b. Negative Signs: If either snake displays aggression, separate them immediately. Signs of aggression include hissing, striking, or biting. Try reintroducing them after a few days.

Courtship and Mating Behaviors

Once the male and female are introduced, they will exhibit specific behaviors that indicate courtship and mating. Understanding these behaviors helps you determine if the pairing is successful.

1. Courtship Behavior:

a. Male Behavior: The male will actively pursue the female, rubbing his head and body against her. He may also exhibit "spurring," where he uses his vestigial leg spurs to stimulate the female.

b.   Female Behavior: The female will generally remain relatively still, but if she is receptive, she may lift her tail slightly, allowing the male to align with her cloaca.

2.   Alignment and Copulation:

a.   Alignment: The male will align his body alongside the female, attempting to position his tail near hers.

b.   Copulation: When the male successfully aligns, he will insert one of his hemipenes into the female's cloaca. This process can take several hours to ensure successful fertilization.

3. Post-Mating Behavior: After copulation, the male may remain in the female's enclosure for several days to repeat the mating process. Multiple matings can increase the chances of successful fertilization.

Monitoring Mating Success

After observing courtship and mating, it's essential to monitor the success of the breeding efforts. This involves looking for signs of successful mating and ensuring the health and well-being of both snakes.

1. Separation: After a few days of observed mating, separate the male from the female to prevent stress and allow the female to focus on developing her eggs. Repeat introductions can be

done every few weeks to ensure successful fertilization.

2.   Signs of Successful Mating: Look for behavioral and physical signs that indicate successful mating.

a.   Female Behavior: The female may become less active and start showing nesting behaviors, such as seeking out the warm side of the enclosure and preparing a nesting spot.

b.   Physical Changes: As the eggs develop, the female will gain weight, and her midsection may appear swollen. This is often noticeable a few weeks after successful mating.

3.   Ovulation: A clear sign of successful mating is ovulation, where the female's body swells significantly

due to the developing eggs. This swelling usually lasts for a few days.

4.   Pre-Lay Shed: Approximately two weeks after ovulation, the female will undergo a pre-lay shed. This is a good indication that she will lay eggs soon. After shedding, she will typically lay eggs within 2-4 weeks.

5.   Post-Mating Care: Ensure both snakes receive appropriate care after mating.

a.   Female: Provide a nesting box with appropriate substrate for the female to lay her eggs. Maintain optimal humidity and temperature levels to support her through this process.

b.   Male: Allow the male to rest and regain his strength. Continue regular feeding and monitor his health.

6.   Egg Laying and Incubation: Once the female lays her eggs, carefully collect them and transfer them to an incubator. Maintain consistent temperature and humidity in the incubator to ensure successful development and hatching.

CHAPTER SIX

EGG LAYING AND INCUBATION

Breeding ball pythons requires careful attention to the period following mating, during which the female prepares to lay eggs. Understanding the steps involved in post-mating care, recognizing signs of gravidity, preparing for egg laying, handling the eggs properly, and setting up the incubation environment is crucial for successful breeding.

Post-Mating Care

Once mating is complete, it's essential to focus on the care of both the female and male ball pythons.

1. Female Care:

a. Nutrition: Continue feeding the female regularly, but be mindful of her appetite, which might decrease as she gets closer to laying eggs.

b. Environment: Maintain optimal conditions in the enclosure with appropriate temperature gradients and humidity levels.

c. Hydration: Ensure the female has constant access to fresh water, as hydration is crucial for egg development.

2. Male Care:

a. Rest and Recovery: After mating, give the male a period of rest and continue to provide regular feeding and proper care.

Signs of Gravidity

Gravidity refers to the state of being pregnant with eggs. Recognizing the signs of gravidity will help you anticipate when the female is ready to lay eggs.

1.   Behavioral Changes: A gravid female may become less active and spend more time coiled in a secure location within her enclosure.

2.   Physical Changes: Look for swelling in the midsection of the female's body. This swelling will become more pronounced as the eggs develop.

3.   Pre-Lay Shed: Approximately two weeks after ovulation, the female will undergo a shed. This is a clear sign that she is preparing to lay eggs soon.

Preparing for Egg Laying

As the female approaches egg-laying, it's important to prepare her environment to support the process.

1.   Nesting Box: Provide a nesting box with an appropriate substrate, such as damp sphagnum moss or vermiculite, to help maintain humidity and give the female a suitable place to lay her eggs.

2.   Temperature and Humidity: Maintain a warm side of the enclosure at around 88-90°F and a cooler side at around 80°F. Keep humidity levels between 50-60%, but slightly higher in the nesting box.

3.   Monitoring: Regularly check on the female to ensure she is comfortable and

has a secure, quiet environment for laying her eggs.

Egg Collection and Handling

Once the female lays her eggs, proper collection and handling are essential to ensure the eggs develop correctly.

1.   Timing: Check the nesting box daily as the expected laying date approaches. Females typically lay eggs within 2-4 weeks after the pre-lay shed.

2.   Collection: Carefully remove the female from the nesting box once you see the eggs. Be gentle to avoid stressing her.

3.   Handling Eggs: Gently lift the eggs, keeping them in the same orientation as they were laid to avoid disrupting the developing embryos. Place the eggs in

an incubation container with a suitable incubation medium, such as vermiculite or perlite, mixed with water to maintain humidity.

INCUBATION SETUP AND MANAGEMENT

Creating the right environment in the incubator is crucial for the development of the eggs.

Temperature and Humidity Control

1.   Temperature: Maintain   a consistent temperature in the incubator between   88-90°F.   Fluctuations   in temperature can negatively affect the development of the embryos.

2.   Humidity: Keep humidity levels between 90-100%. Use a hygrometer to

monitor humidity and add water to the incubation medium as needed to maintain the correct levels.

Incubation Methods

Several incubation methods can be used to ensure successful egg development:

1. Substrate-Based Incubation: This involves placing the eggs on a damp incubation medium, such as vermiculite or perlite. Mix the medium with water in a 1:1 ratio by weight to maintain proper humidity.

2. Suspension Incubation: In this method, the eggs are placed on a grate or suspended above water to maintain high humidity. This can prevent issues related to substrate moisture levels.

3. Container Setup: Use a plastic container with a secure lid to house the eggs during incubation. Ensure the container has ventilation holes to allow for air exchange.

CHAPTER SEVEN

HATCHING AND NEONATE CARE

Successfully hatching ball python eggs and caring for the newborns (neonates) involves recognizing the signs of imminent hatching, assisting with difficult hatches, managing the first shed and first feed, and properly housing the hatchlings. Here's a detailed guide to help you through these crucial steps.

Signs of Imminent Hatching

As the incubation period comes to an end, typically around 55-60 days, you'll notice signs indicating that hatching is about to occur.

1.   Dimpling of Eggs: The eggs will begin to dimple or collapse slightly. This is normal and indicates that the

embryos are absorbing the last of the egg's moisture in preparation for hatching.

2.   Pipping: The most obvious sign is pipping, where the baby snakes use their egg tooth to cut through the eggshell. You'll see tiny heads poking out of the eggs as they take their first breaths.

3.   Movement: Increased movement inside the eggs is a sign that the hatchlings are getting ready to emerge.

Assisting Difficult Hatches

Most hatchlings will emerge from their eggs without assistance, but occasionally, some may need a little help.

1.   Patience: Allow 24-48 hours for the hatchlings to emerge on their own after

pipping. This process allows them to absorb the remaining yolk fully.

2.   Intervention: If after 48 hours, a hatchling is struggling or not making progress, you may need to assist. Here's how:

a.   Clean Hands: Always wash your hands thoroughly before handling eggs or hatchlings to avoid introducing bacteria.

b.   Gentle Opening: Carefully peel back a small portion of the eggshell around the pipped area using clean, blunt-tipped scissors or tweezers. Avoid disturbing the membrane as much as possible.

c.   Observation: After partially opening the egg, observe the hatchling.

If it's still absorbing the yolk, give it more time. If necessary, you can open the egg further but avoid removing the hatchling unless it's absolutely necessary for its survival.

3.   Hydration: Ensure the humidity in the incubator remains high during this time to prevent the membranes from drying out.

First Shed and First Feed

After hatching, the newborn ball pythons will undergo their first shed and have their first meal.

1.   First Shed: The first shed usually occurs within 7-10 days after hatching. During this time:

a.   Humidity: Maintain high humidity in the hatchlings' enclosure to aid in the shedding process.

b.   Monitoring: Watch for signs of shedding, such as dulling of the skin and cloudy eyes. After shedding, the hatchlings' colors will become vibrant and clear.

2.   First Feed: After the first shed, the hatchlings are ready for their first meal.

a.   Feeding Prey: Offer appropriately sized prey, typically pinky mice or rat pups. The prey should be about the same width as the hatchling's body.

b.   Feeding Schedule: Feed the hatchlings once a week initially. Some hatchlings may take their first meal without issue, while others might need some encouragement. If a hatchling refuses to eat, wait a few days and try again.

Housing Hatchlings

Proper housing is essential to ensure the health and well-being of the hatchlings.

1.   Enclosure: Use small, secure enclosures such as plastic tubs or small glass tanks to house the hatchlings. Smaller spaces help the hatchlings feel secure and reduce stress.

a.   Size: An enclosure measuring about 6-12 quarts is suitable for hatchlings.

b.   Lids: Ensure the enclosure has a secure lid to prevent escapes.

2.   Substrate: Choose a substrate that is easy to clean and helps maintain humidity.

a.   Paper Towels: Simple and easy to clean, making it easy to monitor the hatchlings' health and waste.

b.   Coconut Husk or Aspen Bedding: These substrates can help with humidity but need to be monitored to avoid mold growth.

3.   Temperature and Humidity: Maintain proper temperature and humidity in the hatchlings' enclosure.

a.   Temperature: Provide a temperature gradient with a warm side at 88-90°F and a cool side at 78-80°F.

b.	Humidity: Keep humidity levels between 50-60%. Increase humidity during shedding periods.

4.	Hides and Water: Ensure each hatchling has access to a hide and a shallow water dish.

a.	Hides: Provide small hiding spots where the hatchlings can feel secure.

b.	Water: Ensure a shallow water dish is always available for drinking and soaking.

5.	Monitoring Health: Regularly check the hatchlings for signs of health issues.

a.	Feeding: Monitor their feeding behavior and ensure they are eating regularly.

b.   Shedding: Ensure   they   are shedding properly without retained skin.

c.   Activity: Observe   their   activity levels and overall behavior to catch any potential health issues early.

CHAPTER EIGHT

GENETICS AND MORPHS

Understanding the genetics and morphs of ball pythons is essential for breeding and predicting the appearance of offspring. This involves learning basic genetic principles, identifying common and rare morphs, breeding for specific traits, and predicting the morphs of the hatchlings.

Basic Genetics Principles

Genetics is the study of heredity and the variation of inherited characteristics. In ball pythons, understanding genetics helps breeders predict the appearance of the offspring based on the genetic makeup of the parents.

1.	Genes and Alleles:

a.   Genes are segments of DNA that determine specific traits.

b.   Alleles are different versions of a gene. Each trait is controlled by two alleles, one inherited from each parent.

2.   Dominant and Recessive Traits:

a.   Dominant Traits: Only one dominant allele is needed for the trait to be expressed. For example, if a ball python inherits a dominant allele for a certain color from one parent, it will display that color.

b.   Recessive Traits: Both alleles must be recessive for the trait to be expressed. If a ball python inherits a recessive allele from both parents, it will display the recessive trait.

3.   Heterozygous and Homozygous:

a.   Heterozygous: The ball python has one dominant and one recessive allele for a trait (e.g., Pp).

b.   Homozygous: The ball python has two identical alleles, either both dominant (PP) or both recessive (pp).

Common and Rare Morphs

Morphs are variations in the appearance of ball pythons, such as color, pattern, and size, caused by genetic differences. Some morphs are common, while others are rare and sought after by breeders.

1.   Common Morphs:

a.   Normal/Wild Type: The typical coloration found in the wild, with brown and black patterns.

b.   Albino: Lack of melanin, resulting in a yellow and white appearance.

c.   Piebald: Patches of normal color mixed with large white areas.

d.   Spider: A distinct pattern with reduced side patterning and wavy lines.

2.   Rare Morphs:

a.   Clown: A unique pattern with a reduced, clean look and a head stamp.

b.   Axanthic: Lacking yellow pigment, resulting in a silver, gray, and black appearance.

c.   Banana/Coral Glow: Bright yellow and orange coloration with lavender spots.

d.   GHI (Gotta Have It): Dark coloration with busy, high-contrast patterns.

Breeding for Specific Traits

Breeding ball pythons for specific traits involves selecting parents with desired genetic qualities to produce offspring with those traits.

1. Selective Breeding: Choosing parents that display the desired traits and have the appropriate genetic makeup. For example, to breed albino ball pythons, both parents must carry the recessive albino gene.

2. Line Breeding: Breeding related animals to enhance specific traits. This can fix desirable traits but also increases the risk of genetic defects.

3. Outcrossing: Introducing unrelated individuals to increase genetic diversity and reduce the risk of defects. This is

often done to strengthen a particular morph.

Predicting Offspring Morphs

Predicting the morphs of the offspring involves understanding the genetic makeup of the parents and using genetic principles to forecast the possible outcomes.

1. Punnett Squares: A tool used to predict the probability of offspring inheriting specific traits based on the genetic makeup of the parents. Each square represents a possible genetic combination.

a. Example: If both parents are heterozygous for a trait (Pp), the Punnett square will show the probabilities of the offspring being PP, Pp, or pp.

2.   Genotype and Phenotype:

a.   Genotype: The genetic makeup of an individual (e.g., Pp for a heterozygous albino).

b.   Phenotype: The   physical appearance resulting from the genotype (e.g., an albino snake if the genotype is pp).

3.   Probability   Calculations: By understanding   the   dominant   and recessive nature of the genes involved, you can calculate the likelihood of various   morphs   appearing   in   the offspring.

a.   Example: Breeding   two heterozygous albino snakes (Pp x Pp) gives a 25% chance of producing a homozygous albino (pp).

CHAPTER NINE

HEALTH AND DISEASE MANAGEMENT

Maintaining the health of ball pythons is essential for successful breeding and overall well-being. This involves being aware of common health issues in breeding, implementing preventive health care measures, recognizing and treating illnesses promptly, and accessing veterinary care and resources when needed.

Common Health Issues in Breeding

Breeding ball pythons can be susceptible to various health issues, including:

1. Respiratory Infections: Caused by bacterial or fungal pathogens, respiratory infections can result from

inadequate husbandry, such as incorrect temperature or humidity levels.

2.   Mites and Ticks: External parasites can infest ball pythons, causing irritation, anemia, and potential secondary infections.

3.   Internal Parasites: Worms and other internal parasites can affect ball pythons, particularly those that are wild-caught or have been exposed to contaminated prey.

4.   Egg-Binding: Female ball pythons may experience difficulty laying eggs, leading to a potentially life-threatening condition if not addressed promptly.

5.   Scale Rot: A bacterial infection that affects the scales, often resulting from

prolonged exposure to damp substrate or unsanitary conditions.

6. Neurological Issues: Certain morphs, such as spider ball pythons, may be prone to neurological abnormalities that affect their coordination and mobility.

Preventive Health Care

Preventive health care measures are crucial for minimizing the risk of health issues and maintaining the well-being of ball pythons.

1. Proper Husbandry: Ensure the enclosure provides appropriate temperature gradients, humidity levels, and clean water. Regularly clean and disinfect the enclosure to prevent the buildup of bacteria and parasites.

2. Quarantine New Additions: Quarantine new ball pythons for at least 60-90 days before introducing them to your breeding collection. This helps prevent the spread of diseases to established snakes.

3. Regular Health Checks: Monitor your ball pythons regularly for signs of illness or injury, including changes in appetite, behavior, or appearance.

4. Parasite Control: Routinely check for external parasites such as mites and ticks and treat promptly if detected. Administer deworming medication as recommended by a veterinarian to control internal parasites.

5. Proper Nutrition: Provide a balanced diet consisting of appropriately

sized prey items and supplement as needed to ensure optimal nutrition.

Recognizing and Treating Illnesses

Prompt recognition and treatment of illnesses are essential for minimizing the impact on the health and well-being of ball pythons.

1.   Signs of Illness: Be vigilant for signs of illness, including:

a.   Respiratory Issues: Wheezing, open-mouth breathing, or excess mucus.

b.   Behavioral Changes: Decreased activity, loss of appetite, or abnormal posture.

c.   Physical Symptoms: Skin lesions, swelling, or abnormalities in the eyes or mouth.

2. Isolation: If you suspect a ball python is sick, isolate it from other snakes to prevent potential transmission of disease.

3. Consult a Veterinarian: Seek veterinary care promptly if you suspect your ball python is ill. A reptile veterinarian can provide an accurate diagnosis and recommend appropriate treatment.

4. Treatment: Follow your veterinarian's treatment plan carefully, which may include medication, supportive care, or environmental adjustments.

5. Quarantine: If a ball python is diagnosed with a contagious illness, quarantine it from other snakes until it

has fully recovered to prevent spreading the infection.

Vet Care and Resources

Accessing veterinary care and resources is essential for addressing health issues and ensuring the well-being of ball pythons.

1.   Find a Reptile Veterinarian: Locate a qualified reptile veterinarian in your area who has experience treating ball pythons. They can provide routine health checks, diagnostic tests, and treatment for illnesses.

2.   Emergency Care: Identify emergency veterinary clinics or hospitals that are equipped to handle reptile emergencies, especially outside regular business hours.

3. Educational Resources: Stay informed about ball python health care by reading reputable books, articles, and online resources. Joining online forums or communities of experienced reptile keepers can also provide valuable insights and support.

CHAPTER TEN

ETHICS AND BEST PRACTICES IN BALL PYTHON BREEDING

Maintaining high ethical standards and following best practices are essential for responsible ball python breeding. This involves ensuring responsible breeding practices, promoting genetic diversity, adhering to legal considerations and permits, and conducting ethical sales and shipping procedures.

Responsible Breeding Practices

Responsible breeding practices prioritize the health and well-being of the ball pythons and aim to produce healthy offspring while minimizing negative impacts on the breeding population and the environment.

1. Selective Pairing: Breeding should involve selecting pairs with complementary traits to produce healthy and genetically diverse offspring. Avoid pairing individuals with known health issues or genetic defects.

2. Health Screening: Before breeding, conduct thorough health screenings to ensure that breeding snakes are free from diseases, parasites, and genetic abnormalities.

3. Proper Husbandry: Provide optimal living conditions for breeding snakes, including appropriate enclosure setups, temperature gradients, humidity levels, and nutritious diets.

4. Responsible Selling: Screen potential buyers to ensure they have the

knowledge, resources, and commitment to care for the ball pythons properly. Provide educational resources and ongoing support to new owners.

Genetic Diversity and Avoiding Inbreeding

Maintaining genetic diversity is crucial for the long-term health and viability of ball python populations. Breeding practices should aim to preserve genetic diversity and avoid inbreeding, which can lead to health problems and genetic defects.

1. Outcrossing: Introduce unrelated individuals into breeding programs to increase genetic diversity and reduce the risk of inbreeding depression.

2.   Line Breeding: While line breeding can fix desirable traits, it should be done cautiously to avoid excessive inbreeding and the associated risks.

3.   Genetic Testing: Use genetic testing to assess the relatedness of breeding pairs and identify potential genetic issues before breeding.

4.   Breeding Records: Keep detailed records of breeding pairings, offspring, and genetic lineage to track genetic diversity and avoid unintentional inbreeding.

Legal Considerations and Permits

Breeding and selling ball pythons may be subject to legal regulations and permitting requirements, depending on your location. It's essential to understand and comply with relevant laws and obtain any necessary permits or licenses.

1. Research Local Laws: Familiarize yourself with the laws and regulations governing the breeding, sale, and ownership of ball pythons in your area. This includes regulations related to species conservation, exotic animal permits, and breeding permits.

2. Obtain Permits: If required, obtain any necessary permits or licenses for breeding, selling, or transporting ball pythons. Follow proper procedures for permit applications and ensure compliance with permit conditions.

3. Ethical Considerations: Even if not legally required, ethical considerations

may dictate obtaining permits or adhering to specific breeding and selling practices to promote responsible stewardship of ball python populations.

Selling and Shipping Ball Pythons

Ethical selling and shipping practices prioritize the welfare of the ball pythons and ensure their safe and humane transport to new homes.

1. Transparent Sales Practices: Provide accurate and honest information about the health, genetics, and history of the ball pythons being sold. Disclose any known health issues, genetic traits, or previous breeding history.

2. Safe Shipping Procedures: When shipping ball pythons to buyers, use

appropriate shipping containers, packing materials, and shipping methods to ensure the safety and well-being of the animals during transport.

3. Temperature Regulation: Monitor and regulate temperature conditions during shipping to prevent temperature extremes that could harm the ball pythons.

4. Customer Education: Provide educational resources and guidance to buyers on proper care, handling, and husbandry requirements for ball pythons. Offer ongoing support and assistance to help new owners successfully care for their new pets.

CHAPTER ELEVEN

ADVANCED BREEDING TECHNIQUES

Advanced breeding techniques in ball python breeding involve strategic approaches to achieve specific breeding goals, promote genetic diversity, and produce desirable morphs. These techniques include selective breeding strategies, line breeding and outcrossing, advanced genetic projects, and comprehensive record-keeping and data analysis.

Selective Breeding Strategies

Selective breeding involves carefully choosing breeding pairs based on specific traits to enhance and refine desirable characteristics in offspring.

1.   Trait Selection: Identify the traits you want to improve or introduce in your breeding program, such as color, pattern, size, or temperament.

2.   Pedigree Analysis: Analyze the genetic lineage of potential breeding pairs to identify individuals with the desired traits and genetic diversity.

3.   Breeding Goals: Define clear breeding goals and objectives to guide your selective breeding efforts. This may include producing specific morphs, improving color intensity, or eliminating undesirable traits.

4.   Continual Evaluation: Regularly evaluate the offspring produced by selective breeding to assess progress

towards breeding goals and make adjustments as needed.

Line Breeding and Outcrossing

Line breeding and outcrossing are breeding methods used to manipulate genetic traits and maintain genetic diversity within a breeding population.

1.   Line Breeding: In line breeding, closely related individuals, such as siblings or offspring and parents, are bred together to reinforce desirable traits and establish a distinct genetic line. Care must be taken to avoid excessive inbreeding and the associated risks of genetic defects.

2.   Outcrossing: Outcrossing involves breeding unrelated individuals to introduce genetic diversity and

minimize the risks of inbreeding depression. Outcrossing can help strengthen existing genetic lines and introduce new traits into a breeding program.

3. Balancing Line Breeding and Outcrossing: Successful breeding programs often incorporate a balance of line breeding and outcrossing to maintain genetic diversity while selectively breeding for specific traits.

Advanced Genetic Projects

Advanced genetic projects involve targeted breeding efforts to produce new and unique morphs, explore genetic interactions, and advance the understanding of ball python genetics.

1. Morph Development: Breeders may focus on creating new morphs by combining existing morphs or identifying and developing new genetic mutations.

2. Genetic Research: Conducting genetic research and experiments to study inheritance patterns, gene interactions, and the underlying mechanisms of morph development.

3. Collaboration: Collaborate with other breeders, geneticists, and researchers to exchange knowledge, share resources, and collaborate on advanced genetic projects.

4. Ethical Considerations: Exercise caution and ethical responsibility when conducting advanced genetic projects to

ensure the health and welfare of the animals involved and promote the long-term sustainability of ball python breeding.

Record Keeping and Data Analysis

Comprehensive record-keeping and data analysis are essential for tracking breeding outcomes, evaluating breeding strategies, and making informed decisions in a breeding program.

1. Breeding Records: Maintain detailed records of breeding pairings, offspring produced, genetic traits, morphs, health information, and other relevant data.

2. Pedigree Analysis: Analyze pedigree data to assess genetic

relationships, identify genetic trends, and make informed decisions about future breeding pairings.

3. Data Analysis Tools: Utilize software programs or databases designed for breeding record-keeping and data analysis to organize and analyze breeding data effectively.

4. Continuous Improvement: Regularly review and analyze breeding data to evaluate breeding strategies, identify areas for improvement, and refine breeding goals and objectives.

CHAPTER TWELVE

TROUBLESHOOTING AND FAQS IN BALL PYTHON BREEDING

Troubleshooting common breeding problems and addressing frequently asked questions (FAQs) are essential aspects of successful ball python breeding. By understanding common issues and providing clear answers to common questions, breeders can overcome challenges and support the success of their breeding endeavors.

Common Breeding Problems and Solutions

1. Difficulty Breeding: If breeding attempts are unsuccessful, consider factors such as the age and health of the breeding pair, environmental conditions, and timing. Adjusting

temperature, humidity, and photoperiod may help stimulate breeding behavior.

2. Egg-Binding: Egg-binding, or dystocia, can occur when a female has difficulty laying eggs. Provide a warm, humid environment and gentle massage to help the female pass the eggs. If unsuccessful, seek veterinary assistance immediately.

3. Infertile Eggs: Infertile eggs may result from breeding pairs that are incompatible, improper mating techniques, or health issues. Conduct thorough health screenings and consider changing breeding pairs if infertility persists.

4. Incubation Issues: Incubation problems, such as fluctuating

temperatures or improper humidity levels, can affect egg viability. Monitor and adjust the incubation environment to ensure optimal conditions for embryo development.

5. Hatchling Health: Monitor hatchlings closely for signs of dehydration, malnutrition, or health issues. Provide appropriate housing, nutrition, and veterinary care to promote hatchling health and development.

Frequently Asked Questions

1. How often should I breed my ball pythons?

a. Breeding frequency depends on various factors, including the age, health, and breeding history of the snakes. Generally, ball pythons can be bred once per year, but it's essential to monitor the health and condition of the breeding pair.

2.   How do I know if my ball python is ready to breed?

a.   Signs of breeding readiness include increased appetite, weight gain in females, and mating behaviors such as male combat and courtship rituals. Consult with experienced breeders or a veterinarian for guidance on determining breeding readiness.

3.   What should I feed breeding ball pythons?

a.   Provide a balanced diet of appropriately sized prey items, such as mice or rats, to breeding ball pythons.

Offer prey items every 1-2 weeks, adjusting feeding frequency and prey size based on the individual snake's needs.

4. How do I prevent inbreeding in my breeding program?

a. To avoid inbreeding, maintain detailed breeding records, track genetic lineages, and avoid repeated pairings of closely related individuals. Incorporate outcrossing and genetic diversity into your breeding program to mitigate the risk of inbreeding depression.

5. How do I ship ball pythons safely?

a. When shipping ball pythons, use insulated shipping containers equipped with heat or cold packs, depending on weather conditions. Ensure proper ventilation, secure packaging, and timely delivery to minimize stress and ensure the safety of the snakes during transit.

6. What should I do if my ball python refuses to eat during breeding season?

a. It's not uncommon for ball pythons to lose their appetite during breeding season. Provide a quiet, stress-free environment, offer food regularly, and monitor the snake's weight and condition. If feeding issues persist, consult with a veterinarian to rule out any underlying health concerns.

THE END

www.ingramcontent.com/pod-product-compliance
Lightning Source LLC
Chambersburg PA
CBHW061246250726
48653CB00002B/530